MORE THAN A GAME

COURAGE
ON THE FOOTBALL FIELD

AND OTHER
FOOTBALL SKILLS

by Elliott Smith

CAPSTONE PRESS
a capstone imprint

Published by Capstone Press, an imprint of Capstone.
1710 Roe Crest Drive
North Mankato, Minnesota 56003
capstonepub.com

SPORTS ILLUSTRATED KIDS is a trademark of ABG-SI LLC. Used with permission.

Library of Congress Cataloging-in-Publication Data
Names: Smith, Elliott, author.
Title: Courage on the football field : and other football skills / by Elliott Smith.
Description: North Mankato, Minnesota : Capstone Captivate is published by Capstone Press, [2022]
| Series: Sports Illustrated Kids: More than a game | Includes bibliographical references and index. |
Audience: Ages 8–11 years | Audience: Grades 4–6 | Summary: "Today's football superstars know it takes talent, skill, courage, and perseverance to make them great on the gridiron. This Sports Illustrated Kids title combines fast-paced action, famous plays, and SEL skills to show what sets your favorite athletes and teams apart-on and off the field"—Provided by publisher.
Identifiers: LCCN 2021002804 (print) | LCCN 2021002805 (ebook) | ISBN 9781663906717 (Hardcover) |
ISBN 9781663920614 (Paperback) | ISBN 9781663906687 (PDF) | ISBN 9781663906700 (Kindle Edition)
Subjects: LCSH: Football—United States—Juvenile literature. | Football—Training—Juvenile literature.
| Football for children—Juvenile literature.
Classification: LCC GV950.7 .S586 2021 (print) | LCC GV950.7 (ebook) | DDC 796.330973—dc23
LC record available at https://lccn.loc.gov/2021002804
LC ebook record available at https://lccn.loc.gov/2021002805

Editorial Credits
Editor: Alison Deering; Designer: Heidi Thompson; Media Researcher: Morgan Walters;
Production Specialist: Tori Abraham

Image Credits
Associated Press: Jacques Boissinot/The Canadian Press, 27, Mark Humphrey, 26, Mark Tenally, 8, Todd Rosenberg, (left) Cover, 29; Getty Images: Michael Reaves, 16, skynesher, 4; Newscom: MSA/Icon Sportswire, 25, Rich Graessle/Icon Sportswire CGV, 24, Sean Brown/Cal Sport Media, 7; Shutterstock: 135pixels, (bottom right) Cover, Avector, (dots) design element, Christopher Lyzcen, 5, Cynthia Farmer, (middle right) Cover, EFKS, (arena) design element, Flamingo Images, (top middle) Cover; Sports Illustrated: Al Tielemans, 19, Erick W. Rasco, 6, 10, 11, 14, 15, 20, 21, 23, Robert Beck, 9, 12, 13, 22

All internet sites appearing in back matter were available and accurate when this book was sent to press.

TABLE OF CONTENTS

Glossary terms are **BOLD** on first use.

EVERY YARD COUNTS

Football is a tough game. It requires speed, strength, and smarts to succeed. But football also teaches both social and emotional skills. Those are equally important for both young athletes and professional players.

From flag football to the National Football League (NFL), players must learn how to work together and develop good relationships. They learn how to set and achieve positive goals. And athletes must manage their emotions during the highs and lows of the sport.

The challenges are difficult. But the best athletes, teams, and coaches demonstrate how **perseverance**, strength, and hard work create winners on and off the gridiron.

PERSEVERANCE

One critical skill football teaches is perseverance. Players must be able to bounce back from hard hits. Running backs must grind through one- or two-yard carries until they break free. The ability to work through challenges despite difficulty is a key trait in successful football players.

Shaquem Griffin (left) of the Seattle Seahawks rushes a Philadelphia Eagles player.

Brothers—and teammates—Shaquem and Shaquill Griffin embrace before a game.

Ability, Not Disability

When linebacker Shaquem Griffin was 4 years old, he was in severe pain from a serious medical condition. Doctors were forced to remove his left hand. That could have ended his NFL dreams. But Griffin never stopped believing—or playing sports.

Alongside his twin brother, Shaquill, Griffin competed in football, baseball, and track. He became a superstar linebacker at the University of Central Florida (UCF). But when it came time for the NFL, Griffin still had to prove himself.

He performed well at pre-**draft** workouts. Later, he was selected by the Seattle Seahawks in the fifth round of the 2018 NFL draft. Griffin and his brother played together on the Seahawks team for three seasons.

A Remarkable Comeback

In a November 2018 game, NFL quarterback Alex Smith suffered a horrible leg injury. An infection in his fractured leg almost cost Smith his life. After a career that included throwing for more than 34,000 yards and 190 touchdowns, the QB was at risk to never walk again.

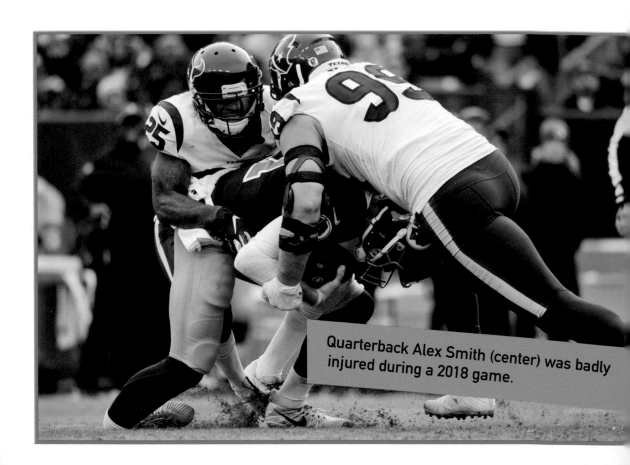

Quarterback Alex Smith (center) was badly injured during a 2018 game.

Smith endured 17 surgeries on his right leg and spent months in the hospital. But the desire to play was still there. Smith beat the odds. He began walking without assistance. He decided that his football career was not over.

Almost two years after the accident, Smith walked onto the field once again to play quarterback. It was one of the most remarkable comebacks in NFL history and a display of strength on and off the field.

Smith started six games for Washington in 2020 and led the team to the playoffs. "I'm grateful to be here today," Smith said.

Smith threw the ball in 2013, prior to his injury.

James Conner runs the ball for the Pittsburgh Steelers.

Conner Beats Cancer

Football teaches perseverance both in the game and in life. While playing college football at the University of Pittsburgh, running back James Conner hurt his knee. During a scan, doctors discovered Conner had Hodgkin's lymphoma. If it had gone undiscovered, the cancer would have eventually killed him.

Conner battled through difficult chemotherapy sessions. He never stopped thinking he would return to football. In 2016, he was declared cancer-free. A year later, after one final college season, he was drafted by the Pittsburgh Steelers.

Now the team's starting running back, Conner is an **advocate** for others dealing with cancer. He hosts patients at games and makes visits to local hospitals.

Connor received a handoff during a 2020 game.

TEAMWORK AND INCLUSIVITY

The people involved in a football game have different skills and knowledge. For those on the field and on the sidelines, teamwork and inclusivity are key. Players, coaches, and officials learn to appreciate their differences and come together to create an environment that helps make the game better.

The New England Patriots' Julian Edelman (11) in action during Super Bowl LI

Edelman passes the ball in Super Bowl LI.

A Super Bowl to Remember

Super Bowl LI, played on February 5, 2017, was a tense game. After falling behind 28–3 to the Atlanta Falcons, the New England Patriots were in trouble. It looked like they were going to get blown out in the biggest game of the year.

But teamwork, communication, and a shared purpose played a major role in New England's historic comeback. The Patriots' offense received huge contributions from wide receiver Julian Edelman. The defense managed critical stops, including a forced **fumble** by Dont'a Hightower.

In all, New England scored 31 straight points—including overtime—for the largest comeback ever in a Super Bowl. The team came together to beat the Falcons 34–28 in a victory to remember.

Breaking Gender Barriers

Just like football is a team sport, so is officiating. Crews typically stay together all season. Teamwork is critical in order to make sure the game is called correctly. It also takes quick thinking and extensive football knowledge to become an NFL official. For Sarah Thomas, a lifelong athlete and football fan, it seemed like a natural fit.

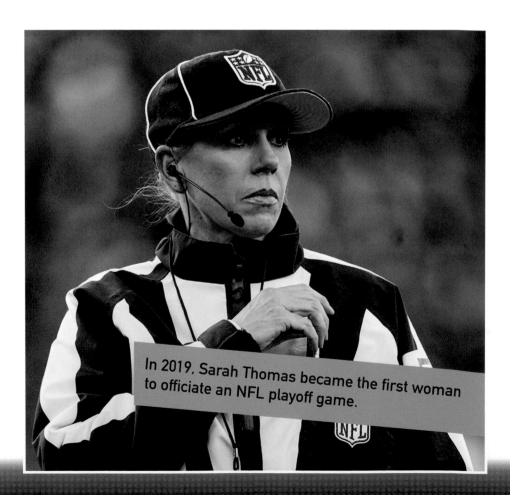

In 2019, Sarah Thomas became the first woman to officiate an NFL playoff game.

Thomas spent years of officiating grade school, high school, and college football games. In 2015, she became the NFL's first full-time female official. As a down judge, Thomas calls **offsides** and other key penalties.

"My goal is to just be the best I can be every time I'm given the opportunity to work," Thomas said.

Making History

In 2021, the NFL announced that Thomas would be the first woman to officiate a Super Bowl game. Thomas served as a down judge at Super Bowl LV in Tampa, Florida.

Thomas made a touchdown call during a 2019 game between the Patriots and the Chargers.

The Miami Miracle

Nearing the end of the 2018 NFL season, the Miami Dolphins needed a win against the New England Patriots. If the Dolphins lost, the Patriots would secure their tenth straight division title.

With seven seconds left in the game, the Dolphins were trailing the Patriots. They needed to go 69 yards for a touchdown. The Dolphins had a "one in a million" chance of winning. It would take teamwork and determination to pull it off.

Ryan Tannehill, quarterback for the Miami Dolphins, gets ready to pass the ball.

Dolphins quarterback Ryan Tannehill threw a quick pass to receiver Kenny Stills. Stills pitched the ball to DeVante Parker, who ran for several yards. Parker then **lateraled** to running back Kenyan Drake.

Down the field, Miami linemen delivered several key blocks. Drake had one man to beat. Patriots tight end Rob Gronkowski took the wrong angle. Drake scooted by him to score, firing the ball in the stands. The Miami Miracle was born.

Impressive Offense

The offensive line is an underrated aspect of football. The five players on the line must work in **tandem** to open holes for running backs or protect the quarterback. One false step or missed assignment could result in a poor play. Building a good relationship helps the line work efficiently.

One of the best offensive lines in football belongs to the Indianapolis Colts. Their five starters have earned numerous awards and the respect of opposing players. Guard Quenton Nelson is the anchor of the line. He specializes in driving defenders down the field with his blocks. Nelson was named All-Pro in 2018 and 2019. He was also named to the Pro Bowl for 2018, 2019, and 2020.

SELF-CONFIDENCE

Playing football at a professional level is extremely difficult. Only a select few players even make it into the NFL. That's why self-confidence is a key element for many players. Having the conviction to keep going in the face of obstacles helps players and coaches beat the odds.

Let Russ Cook

For years, people told 5-foot, 11-inch-tall football star Russell Wilson he was too short to play quarterback. But Wilson was confident in his own talents and abilities. He proved height doesn't matter as much as heart.

In 2012, Wilson was drafted by the Seattle Seahawks and named starting quarterback. Since then, he has carried much of the responsibility for the team on his shoulders. Wilson is the first person to arrive at the practice facility and the last person to leave.

Wilson's hard work has made him a Super Bowl champion. In 2014, he led the Seahawks to victory over the Denver Broncos in Super Bowl XLVIII. And in 2019, he signed a four-year, $140 million contract extension making him the highest-paid player in the league at the time.

Seattle Seahawks quarterback Russell Wilson shows off his throwing skills.

Wilson's ability and self-confidence allow him to make unbelievable throws under pressure. "Do I think I am the best quarterback in the NFL? I believe so, without a doubt," he said.

MVP in the Making

The NFL's Most Valuable Player (MVP) in 2019 had a long road to his success at quarterback. Coaches in college and scouts for the NFL wanted the speedy Lamar Jackson to switch positions to wide receiver. His quickness would have made him hard to stop at receiver as a deep passing threat.

Lamar Jackson in action as quarterback for the Baltimore Ravens

Jackson won his 2019 MVP award by **unanimous** vote. He is only the second player in history, after Tom Brady, to win unanimously.

Jackson passes during a playoff game against the Tennessee Titans.

But Jackson knew he could succeed as a QB. And he had an especially important supporter in his corner—his mother, Felicia Jones, who also serves as his manager. Her confidence helped Jackson stay focused on playing quarterback. He even removed himself from the 40-yard dash during workouts so teams wouldn't consider him as a receiver.

Jackson continues to show why his skills are so important for the Baltimore Ravens. He keeps defenses off-balance with both his running and throwing ability. In his MVP season, he set a record for the most rushing yards in a season by a quarterback. He also threw 36 touchdown passes.

The Undrafted Star

It would have been easy for Austin Ekeler to give up. The running back had several strikes against him in his quest to make it to the NFL. He played at a small college, Western Colorado University. None of the 32 teams in the NFL drafted him. And when he signed with the Los Angeles Chargers as a free agent, he was low on the **depth chart**.

Austin Ekeler rushes for the Los Angeles Chargers.

Ekeler gets tackled by players from the New England Patriots.

But Ekeler's self-confidence fueled him. When he saw the chance to make an impression during a preseason game, he took advantage of it. He made several tackles on special teams. He ran for 50 yards on eight carries. And he caught three passes for 58 yards.

Ekeler's performance—and his versatility—helped him make the team. Now, Ekeler is the Chargers' starting running back. In 2020, he signed a four-year, $24.5 million contract with the team, proving hard work and confidence pay off.

RESPECT, PATIENCE, AND EMPATHY

Football is a lot more than wins and losses or tackles and touchdowns. Earning the respect of peers and players can help a coach's message get through. Staying patient and awaiting an opportunity can help players make a difference on and off the field. And showing **empathy** to those in need can bring teammates closer together.

Katie Sowers is photographed with players from the San Francisco 49ers ahead of Super Bowl LIV.

Breaking Barriers

After finishing her football career as a player in the Women's Football Alliance, Katie Sowers was looking for a new challenge. Through a special NFL program, she began working with the Atlanta Falcons coaches during the 2016 preseason.

Sowers wore a face mask during a 2020 game.

In 2017, Sowers started making history. She was hired to be an offensive assistant by the San Francisco 49ers. She was just the second woman ever to become a full-time coach in the NFL. Sowers didn't stop there. She became the first woman to coach in a Super Bowl game in 2020.

Sowers's hard work and knowledge have earned her the respect of the team. "She's been tremendous," 49ers QB Jimmy Garoppolo said. "Katie is awesome out there."

Sowers played quarterback and defensive back for the Women's Football Alliance. She led the U.S. national team to a gold medal at the Women's World Championships in 2013.

The Football Doctor

It's difficult to play professional football. But to do that and study to become a doctor? That's exactly what Kansas City Chiefs guard Laurent Duvernay-Tardif did. He balanced books and balls to earn his doctorate from McGill University in Canada.

Duvernay-Tardif spread out his final year of medical school over four NFL off-seasons. Now, he is considered one of the top guards in the league. But he is also a man of healing.

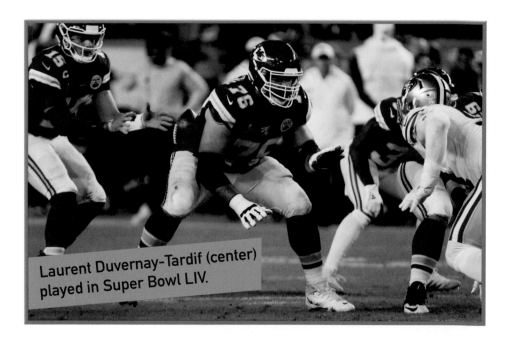

Laurent Duvernay-Tardif (center) played in Super Bowl LIV.

Duvernay-Tardif (center) received the National Assembly of Quebec Medal of Honor in 2020.

In 2020, Duvernay-Tardif sat out the season. In a display of courage and empathy, he chose to use his medical skills to help during the COVID-19 **pandemic**. It earned him a spot as one of *Sports Illustrated*'s Sportspersons of the Year.

Teaming Up for Change

   Social justice issues became important for many athletes in 2020. The deaths of Black men and women, including George Floyd and Breonna Taylor, hit hard for NFL players. Many sought ways to make a difference in their communities.

   Atlanta Falcons player Ricardo Allen is the leader of the team's social justice committee. The group donates and raises money to help support after-school programs in needy neighborhoods. In the summer of 2020, Allen got a call from Falcons quarterback Matt Ryan, who wondered how he could help.

   Allen, Ryan, and the rest of the team came together. They started several **initiatives**, including teaching high school football players in the area about their election rights. The students acted as volunteer poll workers during the 2020 election.

"Turning a blind eye is no longer acceptable to me," Ryan said. "It took time and I wish I had done it faster, but we're in a position where I hope we're starting to move things in the right direction."

Ricardo Allen (left) and Matt Ryan (right) of the Atlanta Falcons are on the team's social justice committee, which Allen founded.

GLOSSARY

advocate (AD-vuh-kuht)—a person who supports an idea or plan

depth chart (DEPTH CHAHRT)—a chart used to show the starting and backup players

draft (DRAFT)—the process of choosing a person to join a sports organization or team

empathy (EM-puh-thee)—imagining how others feel

fumble (FUHM-buhl)—to drop the football while running with it

initiative (ih-NISH-uh-tive)—a first step or movement

lateral (LAT-ur-uhl)—to pass the ball sideways or backward to another player

offside (awf-sahyd)—when the defensive player goes on the offensive side before the ball is snapped

pandemic (pan-DEM-ik)—a disease that spreads over a wide area and affects many people

perseverance (pur-suh-VEER-uhns)—the act of continuing to do something in spite of difficulties

social justice (SOH-shuhl JUHSS-tiss)—equality and fairness for all people in a society

tandem (TAN-dum)—a relationship between two people involving co-operative action

unanimous (yoo-NAN-uh-muhss)—agreed on by everyone

READ MORE

Fuchs, Jeremy, McGarr, Elizabeth, and Page, Sam. *The Greatest Football Teams of All Time: Sports Illustrated Kids*. New York: Time Inc. Books, 2018.

Geoffreys, Clayton. *Russell Wilson: The Inspiring Story of One of Football's Greatest Quarterbacks*. CreateSpace, 2015.

Harts, Shannon H. *Shaquem Griffin: Don't Tell Me What I Can't Do.* New York: PowerKids Press, 2020.

INTERNET SITES

Play Football
playfootball.nfl.com

Sports Illustrated Kids: Football
sikids.com/football

INDEX

COURAGE
ON THE FOOTBALL FIELD
AND OTHER FOOTBALL SKILLS

Today's football superstars know it takes more than talent and skill to stand out. It takes courage and perseverance to be great on the gridiron. Dive into the game with fast-paced action, famous plays, and standout moments, and find out what sets your favorite athletes and teams apart, on and off the field.

MORE THAN A GAME

Some of the best plays of the game involve more than just athletic skills. Sometimes an athlete's social and emotional skills take their sport to a new level. Discover lessons of respect, perseverance, patience, and teamwork through exciting examples from both on and off the field. After all, when it comes to playing a sport, it's often more than game.

BOOKS IN THIS SERIES

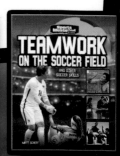

$7.95 US / $9.95 CAN

ISBN 978-1-66392-061-4

capstone
capstonepub.com